THE PÈRE MARQUETTE
LECTURE IN THEOLOGY
1995

THE BOOK OF PROVERBS

AND

OUR SEARCH FOR WISDOM

RICHARD J. CLIFFORD, S.J.
WESTON JESUIT SCHOOL OF THEOLOGY

MARQUETTE UNIVERSITY PRESS
MILWAUKEE, WISCONSIN

Manufactured in the United States of America

ISBN 0-87462-575-0

MARQUETTE UNIVERSITY PRESS
MILWAUKEE

The Association of Jesuit University Presses

The 1995 Père Marquette Lecture in Theology is the twenty-sixth in a series commemorating the missions and explorations of Père Jacques Marquette, S.J. (1637-75). This series of annual lectures was begun in 1969 under the auspices of the Marquette University Department of Theology.

The Joseph A. Auchter Family Endowment Fund has endowed the lecture series. Joseph Auchter (1894-1986), a native of Milwaukee, was a banking and paper industry executive and a long-time supporter of education. The fund was established by his children as a memorial to him.

Father Richard J. Clifford of the Society of Jesus was born in Lewiston, Maine in 1934 and entered the Jesuit order in 1953. He is a graduate of Boston College (A.B.), Weston Jesuit School of Theology (S.T.L.), and Harvard University (Ph.D.). Since his ordination to the Roman Catholic priesthood in 1966, he has taught at Weston School of Theology (now Weston Jesuit School of Theology), including a term as Dean from 1983 to 1987.

Father Clifford was General Editor of the *Catholic Biblical Quarterly* from 1975 to 1980 and also President of the Catholic Biblical Association in 1992. His research interests include the cultural background to the Hebrew Bible, Wisdom Literature, the Psalms and biblical theology. Currently he is writing a commentary on the Book of Proverbs.

Bibliography

"Narrative and Lament in Isaiah 63:7-64:11," in *To Touch the Text: Biblical and Related Studies in Honor of Joseph A. Fitzmyer, S.J.* (ed. M. Horgan and P. Kobelski; N.Y.: Crossroad, 1989) 93-102.

"Psalms as Liturgical Prayer," and "Covenant" in *The New Dictionary of Sacramental Worship* (ed. P. Fink; Wilmington: Glazier, 1990).

"Genesis 1-25" and "Exodus," in *The New Jerome Biblical Commentary*, (Englewood Cliffs: Prentice-Hall, 1989).

"Isaiah 40-66" in *Harper's Bible Dictionary*, (San Francisco: Harper, 1988).

"II Isaiah," in *Anchor Bible Dictionary* (Garden City: Doubleday 1998).

"Genesis 1-3: Permission to Exploit?" *The Bible Today*, 26 (1988) 133-137.

"Mot Invites Baal to a Feast: Observations on a Difficult Ugaritic Text (CTA - KTU 1.5.1)" in *Working with No Data: Thomas Lambdin Festschrift* (Winona Lake: Eisenbrauns, 1986).

"The Hebrew Scriptures and the Theology of Creation," *Theological Studies* 46 (1985) 507-23.

"Cosmogonies in the Ugaritic Texts and in the Bible," *Orientalia* 53 (1984) 183-210.

"The Temple and the Holy Mountain," in *The Temple in Antiquity* (ed. T. Madsen; Provo: Brigham Young, 1984), 107-245.

"In Zion and David A New Beginning: An Interpretation of Psalm 78," in *Traditions and Transformations: Turning Points in Biblical Faith* (eds. B. Halpern and J. Levenson; Winona Lake: Eisebrauns, 1981) 121-41.

"The Bible and the Environment," in *Preserving the Creation: Environmental Theology and Ethics* (Washington, D.C." Georgetown, 1994) 27-32.

"Woman Wisdom in the Book of Proverbs," *Biblische Theologie und gesellschaftlicher Wandel* (Norbert Lohfink volume) (ed., G. Bralik, et al.; Freiburg: Herder, 1993) 61-72.

"Introduction to Wisdom Literature," *New Interpreter's Bible*, 1995.

Project

Commentary on *Proverbs* for the *Old Testament Library*, Westminster Press, Philadelphia (December 1996).

Michel Barnes

THE BOOK OF PROVERBS

AND

OUR SEARCH FOR WISDOM

It is safe to say that the Book of Proverbs is not widely regarded today as a vital part of the Bible and a great resource in living one's life, at least by contemporary North Americans and Europeans. It is not ranked among the top ten, not even among the top forty, of biblical books.[1] Its lack of popularity in North America is particularly striking, given that many of its concerns are those of perennial best sellers by F. Scott Peck, Parker J. Palmer, and others books on finding meaning in life. Themes of contemporary spirituality are everywhere in Proverbs: for example, discernment, making difficult choices, and finding God in all things. Many themes of moral philosophy or theology also appear: Are there any moral absolutes? What is the right thing to do? Will I be punished for bad actions and rewarded for good actions? What do I tell my children about the blessed life?

Interest in these questions runs high in our culture. Many of the topics discussed in afternoon TV shows and radio talk shows are really about being virtuous: how to bear suffering or recover from it; how to accept other people in their differences; how to deal with members of one's family (spouse, children, parents); how to succeed, and how to find and do the right thing. An increasingly important shelf in bookstores is the one called "uplift," "self-help," or "spirituality." These shelves display books on inner serenity, achieving maturity, getting along with other people, becoming a better person, how to cope. Discussion of these topics is sometimes carried on in a theistic framework, but at other times non-theistically.

Obvious and major contextual differences make ancient and modern quests somewhat different, of course: an agricultural versus an industrial economy, a predominantly oral versus a literate society, a religious versus a secular culture, a family-centered view of the human person versus a more individualistic viewpoint. But the similarities far outweigh the differences, making it possible for the seemingly conventional Book of Proverbs to speak authoritatively to us today.

This paper seeks to make the case that the Book of Proverbs is a genuinely religious work lying at the center of the Bible rather than, as is sometimes alleged, a pragmatic and mechanical book at the Bible's fringe. It can speak to us today.

Let us look at the book itself. It is about 930 lines in length, approximately the length of one of the books of Samuel or Kings in the Old Testament, or the Gospel of Matthew in the New. It is an anthology, a cluster of

smaller collections of sayings and instructions that was
edited into a single book.[2]

I. Title and Introduction   1:1-7

II. Instructions of parents and wisdom   1:8-9:18

III. First Solomonic collection of sayings   10:1-22:16

IV. "Sayings of the Wise" instructions partly modeled on
the Egyptian Wisdom of Amenemope   22:17-24:22

V. Further sayings of the wise   24:23-34

VI. Second Solomonic Collection, collected under King
Hezekiah   25-29

VII. Sayings of Agur and other sayings, mostly numerical
30:1-33

VIII. Sayings of King Lemuel, which he got from his
mother   31:1-9

IX. The capable wife   31:10-31

A few questions must be answered before looking
at the contents of Proverbs. When was the book written
and by whom? Scholars generally believe the various
collections of sayings in chapters 10 to 31 were written
sometime between the tenth century B.C. and the sixth
century B.C. exile. The best clue is 25:1: "These too are
proverbs of Solomon, which the men of King Hezekiah
of Judah copied." According to the verse, King Hezekiah
(715-687 B.C.) ordered members of his staff to copy the
sayings of the present chapters 25-29, which were
ascribed to King Solomon, his predecessor of some two
centuries before. Chapters 1-9, which differ in tone and
genre from the rest, are commonly but not universally
judged to have been composed after the Exile as an
introduction to the book. Some feel that the concern in

the book for marrying the right woman reflects the post-exilic concern for proper endogamous marriage attested in the books of Ezra-Nehemiah. Dating Proverbs, it should be said, is risky because sure references to dateable historical events are lacking.

The precise authorship and milieu of the wisdom books are uncertain. There are two theories about how Proverbs arose—the school, sponsored by the king, or the tribe and family. Relying on information from Egypt and Mesopotamia, some scholars suggest that under the monarchy (from the tenth century B.C.) a skilled or "wise" bureaucracy kept records and accounts, handled correspondence with foreign powers and, as part of their duties as court composers and poets, composed Proverbs and other books of the Bible. King Solomon, whose name figures in Proverbs and other wisdom books (Prov 1:1; 10:1, 25:1; Qoh 1:12; Song 1:1; Sir 47:13; Wisdom 7-9) is celebrated in the Bible both for his administration and wisdom (1 Kings 3; 4:29-34; 11:41).

Proponents of the tribal theory point out that the wisdom books do not mention a class of sages. Noting the strong family and tribal traditions of Israel, they trace the admonitions and warnings of the wisdom books to prohibitions laid down by tribal elders that regulated social relations within the tribe. The latter arose from real-life experiences of ordinary people; the sayings were made concise and memorable by the removal of the details of their originating situations.

Unfortunately, lack of information makes it impossible to decide with certainty between the two. In my judgment, royal scribes or poets composed Proverbs, for only they could have read comparable literatures and imitated their genres in Proverbs with such evident skill. Undoubtedly tribal structures played some role since the family was so powerful an institution in Israel, yet it was not the dominant influence. References to rural life and farming in the book of themselves cannot be used as evidence for tribal origins, for they reflect well-nigh universal anxiety about crops and herds in the precarious economy of the ancient world. Comparable agricultural societies in today's world, such as some African societies, may provide hints of the social location of Proverbs; in such societies the king uses appropriate maxims in exercising his rule.

It is time to let the book have its say. As a preliminary step, I want to respond to three common misunderstandings of the book, three reasons for *not* reading Proverbs. These are: (1) it is a book of advice; (2) it is vague and contentless; (3) it is exclusively male in that the book's implied reader is a young man on the threshold of adulthood. I will then speak about three of Proverbs' major contributions to personal religion or spirituality, three reasons *for* reading it: (1) the re-imagining of the moral life that takes place in chapters 1-9; (2) the school of discernment represented by the sayings of chapters 10-31; (3) the New Testament rereading of Proverbs.

The first misunderstanding: (1) Proverbs is a book of advice. Advice is one of these things we quickly get enough of. To be given advice often makes us small and needy, children again. Perhaps for this reason Ambrose Bierce in *The Devil's Dictionary* says that advice is the smallest current coin. Proverbs undoubtedly has many sayings, "proverbs"; even the lengthy instructions in chaps. 1-9 contain aphorisms. But do they give advice? Understanding what a proverb is partially answers the question. Wolfgang Mieder, a paremiologist at the University of Vermont, gives a definition: a proverb is a concise statement of an apparent truth that has currency.[3] Mieder's definition does not win universal acceptance,[4] but provides a good starting point. First, a proverb states a truth; it does not give advice. "A stitch in time saves nine" is not a counsel for aspiring tailors! It rather states in memorable fashion a truth that we almost immediately know is valid. The next phrase in the definition "A concise statement *of an apparent truth*" affirms that the truth of a proverb varies according to the situation. Is the proverb "haste makes waste" more true than "a stitch in time saves nine"? Is "too many cooks spoil the broth" more valid than "many hands make light work"? One must bring the maxim to the situation to determine its fit. Proverbs, then, are not words of advice, but rather theses or statements about reality to bring clarity out of confusion.[5] They invite the reader to become active, to make a judgment, to discern.

(2) A second reason for avoiding Proverbs arises from the vagueness of its teaching. In chapters 1-9, at

least, it does little more than exhort its readers to listen to proper authorities, and to do good and avoid evil. You look in vain for a rule of life, specific axioms to guide you through highs and lows in life, advice on how to raise children or handle money. A full explanation of this phenomenon must await our discussion of Woman Wisdom in the second part of this lecture, but it suffices for now to quote Michael Fox:

> Wisdom...[in chapters 1-9] does not consist simply in knowing what is good to do, such as maintaining sexual virtue and avoiding loan guarantees. Wisdom is a configuration of character, a compound of knowledge, fears, expectations, and desires that enables one to identify the right path and keep to it. Wisdom means not only knowing but also *wanting* to do what is right and to avoid sin. This desire will protect you from the tragic consequences of immorality.[6]

The insistence on character and desire in these chapters explains why specific counsels are not prominent.

(3) The third difficulty the book poses to many modern readers is that its world is male. The implied audience for many of the instructions and sayings is a young man who has left his parents' house to establish his own (especially 1:8-19; 4:1-6). Only to a male would the appeals of Woman Folly and Woman Wisdom be meaningful. In response, we can concede that the author worked within an ancient Palestinian context where young men were the ordinary recipients of instruction. The original audience, however, was never restricted to young men setting out in life. The book itself does not envision them as the sole audience. The introduction (1:1-7) states the intention explicitly,

and the *intention* overrides implicit *assumptions*. To clarify the difference between assumptions and intentions, one may compare the interpretation of apocalyptic language in the New Testament. Some Christian writers, including Paul, assumed on the basis of apocalyptic language an early return of Christ. Their assumption of an early return was gradually reinterpreted or discarded as the Christian community continued through the late first and early second centuries. Proverbs 1:1-7 intends that its readers "...become acquainted with wisdom and instruction, understand learned sayings...." Its audience is not only the "the simple" (= the young, untaught) but also explicitly "the wise" (v. 5), by definition sages who were more experienced, *older*. As regards women, they are included among "the untaught." Moreover, wisdom literature is concerned with the typical. The individual in the sayings and instructions is a type, further reducing the importance of the author's culture-bound assumption of a young man as subject. The major point of chapters 1-9 is the analogy between choosing a life partner and choosing wisdom. And that analogy transcends the original ancient Near Eastern social model. A final and very significant point is that the Bible itself is a library and by that fact "lifts up" all its books to a new dialectical context. The Christian biblical context now includes Gal 3:28, which is explicit about the makeup of the community addressed by the Scriptures: "There is neither Jew nor Greek, there is neither slave nor free person, there is not male and female, for you are all one in Christ Jesus."

Having confronted reasons for not reading Proverbs, we will now look at the positive contributions of the book: (1) chapters 1-9 as a re-imagining of the moral life; (2) chapters 10-31 as a school of discernment; (3) the New Testament rereading.

Part I

Proverbs 1-9 views the moral life far differently from biblical books such as the Pentateuch and the prophets. In the Pentateuch, the law and covenant at Sinai form the basis of morality. God's constant refrain to Moses "You shall say to the Israelites..." confronts community and individual with the divine will. Prominent figures such as Abraham and Sarah, Joseph, and Moses provide examples of righteous conduct. In the prophetic books, the prophets, speaking in the name of God, affirm the ancestral teachings in new situations and show the consequences on national life of the people's conduct and allegiance. Proverbs, however, goes its own way. Its moral route—individual, intellectual, empirical—is not incompatible with the public and nomistic morality of the other books. Both approaches—legal and public, private and reflective—can happily coexist in one and the same person. The variety illustrates the Bible's pluralism, in this case its capacity to conceive morality in different ways.

The opening nine chapters can be analyzed from many angles. I see three distinctive ideas at work: (1) founding a household is a symbol of the moral life; (2) human beings' remarkable liberty of spirit (*disponibilité*) is balanced by the concrete and social results of that liberty; (3) Wisdom is not a series of wise acts but something more, a reality "out there," able to be grasped. (This belief is behind Proverbs' well known personification of wisdom as a woman.)

I.1. Establishing a house is a symbolic expression of the moral life. The opening scene of the book pictures the youth leaving his parental household to make his way in life, to found his own household. As he leaves, his parents plead with him:

[10]My son, if sinners entice you,
  do not go, if they say:
[11]Come with us,
  we will set an ambush for blood,
  lie in wait for the innocent without cause."
[12]We will swallow them alive, like Sheol,
  whole and entire, like those going down to the Pit.
[13]We will obtain all kinds of precious treasure,
  we will fill our houses with the loot.
[14]Throw in your lot with us,
  we all have a single purse."
[15]My son, do not walk on the way with them,
  keep your foot from their path,
[[16]for their feet run to wickedness,
  and they hasten to shed blood;]
[17]for without cause is the net thrown high
  in the sight of a winged creature.
[18]As for them, they are setting an ambush for their own blood,
  lying in wait for their own lives.
[19]Such is the path of everyone greedy for gain;
  it takes the life of its owner.

A preliminary note on v. 16, which is a direct quote from Isa 59:7: as correctly seen by many commentators, it was added by scribes puzzled by verse 17, "for without cause is a net lifted up in the sight of any winged creature." Verse 17 is most probably a passive construction to express divine action. It can be paraphrased: God will not let those walking on evil paths see the net that will entrap them. The passage as a whole says that when young people leave their parents' home, they make a defining choice about the kind of life they will live. In the dramatic perspective of the passage, the choices before the youth are two: the ancestral way represented by the parents, and the way of wrongdoers, here concretely a band of robbers. The wicked invite the young person to join their *community*, "throw in your lot with us, we all have a single purse." The parents recognize that moral decisions are not isolated; rather one chooses in view of a good. In this passage, the "good" is joining a group and sharing its values. At this critical moment in the young person's life the parents exhort their departing offspring to turn a deaf ear to the seductive appeal of that group. The robber band will indeed attain its goal—filling their house with stolen goods—but, ironically, at the cost of their own lives: "Such is the path of everyone greedy for gain; it takes the life of its owner."

The vivid opening scene of the youth leaving home suggests that the context for all subsequent parental exhortations is the same—the moment when young persons leave the parental household to establish themselves through marriage and founding their own house (2; 3:1-12; 4:10-19, 20-27; 5; 6:20-35; and 7). A good

example is chapter 4, where the father uses his own life
as a model for his son.

[1]Heed, O sons, the discipline of a father,
    pay attention to learn discernment,
[2]for beneficial teaching I give you;
    do not turn away from my instruction.
[3]When I was a son with my father,
    tender and beloved before my mother,
[4]he instructed me and said to me:
    "Let your mind hold on to my words.
Guard my commandments and live;
[5]acquire wisdom, acquire understanding!
Do not forget,
    do not deviate from my words.
[6]Do not turn away from her and she will guard you;
    love her and she will protect you.
[7]The beginning of wisdom: acquire wisdom
    and with all your acquisitions acquire insight!
[8]Prize her and she will exalt you;
    she will give you honor if you embrace her.
[9]She will place on your head a graceful necklace,
    a glorious crown she will bestow on you.

The father urges his son to acquire wisdom in language
that is suitable for acquiring a wife. The one verb
"acquire" can mean to acquire wisdom or acquire a
wife. The time of leaving the parental house to found
one's own is full of poignancy, possibility, and danger.
This context adds force and edge to the parental
exhortations. Even the final poem (31:10-31), on the
capable wife, falls within the same context: it shows us
a mature man who has made a successful transition
from his parents home to his own; he has acquired
wisdom and a "capable wife."

The final, and striking, underlining of the moment of leaving one's home and entering another is chapter 9. In that scene, Woman Wisdom invites "simple" youths to come in and partake of the banquet celebrating her new house. It reverses the opening scene of the youth leaving home.

By imaginatively contextualizing moral choice in this fateful transitional moment, the chapter shows how moral choice means establishing one's life, confirms the authority of parental wisdom, and opens the way for the great analogy between searching for a wife and searching for wisdom (I.3 below).

I.2. The second new feature in Proverbs is its twin assumption of great freedom in the disciple *and* its concrete results. In the book, life is action, and the human person is defined through the organs of actions, the organs of perception, decision, expression, and motion, or in the concrete imagery of Proverbs, eye, ear, mouth (tongue, lips), heart, hands, feet. So much stock does Proverbs place in the capacity to direct one's life that it virtually equates knowing the good with doing the good. The ignorance of the fool is not a simple lack of knowledge but an active aversion to it, an aversion arising from cowardice, pride, or laziness of mind. Ignorance has an ethical dimension, and knowing is a moral obligation for human beings. The sage is morally good; the fool is wicked. The book blends ethical and sapiential language in a unique way.

Prov 4:20-27 is a good example of a free and energetic moral agent.

[20]My son, pay attention to my words,
    give your *ear* to my utterances.
[21]Do not let (them) out of your *eye*sight,
    hold them in your *heart*,
[22]for they are life for those who find them,
    healing for his whole body.
[23]More than anything you guard, guard your *heart*,
    for from it comes the source of life.
[24]Rid yourself of a lying *mouth*,
    deceitful *lips* keep far from you.
[25]Keep your *eyes* gazing straight ahead,
    direct your *eyelids* unswervingly before you.
[26]Attend to the path of your *feet*
    so that all your ways turn out well.
[27]Turn neither to the right or the left;
    hold back your *foot* from evil.

The words of the teacher should take root in your heart
to animate you to live rightly. "Heart" designates
"mind" as in Egyptian instructions, i.e., the mind stores
knowledge and is the principle of action. The psychological process described in the piece consists of two
steps: (1) hearing the words of the teacher and treasur-
ing them in the heart as the source of life; (2) speaking,
acting, and walking in accord with the teaching that is
held at the center of one's being. The poem mentions
no less than seven organs of the body—ear, eyes, heart
("mind"), mouth, lips, eyelids, feet (heart, eyes, and feet
are mentioned twice). The disciple is to strain every
sense to its limit (the physical organ stands for the
faculty, e.g., eye for seeing, foot for movement): one is
to "extend" one's ear like an antenna, let nothing escape
the eyes, preserve words in the "heart" (= mind), keep
false speech away from mouth and lips, hold eyes and

eyelids undeviatingly on the goal, keep one's feet from stumbling or taking detours. The teacher assumes to an extraordinary degree that the disciple is free and available.

The mouth (or "tongue" and "lips"), i.e., speech, is the most important of the senses. Through speech, teachers deliver discipline (a word that can mean content or attitude), knowledge, and wisdom. Speech must be truthful and reliable. Lying is strongly denounced (17:4; 19:22; 30:6), particularly lying in the law court (6:19; 12:17; 14:5, 25; 19:5, 9, 28; 21:28). Among the key differences between Woman Wisdom and Folly in chapters 1-9 is the truth or reliability of their words. Metaphors of straight and level, crooked and smooth, describe their discourse. Wisdom says that "none of [my words] are twisted or perverted" (8:8), and "all of them are straight to the intelligent person, on the level to those who have attained knowledge" (8:9). Folly's words, on the other hand, are crooked (5:3; 9:17) or smooth and slippery (2:16; 6:24; 7:5).

Proverbs' well-known annoyance with slackers and the lazy is perhaps best explained as disdain at people's refusal to make use of their freedom.

[6]Go to the ant, O slacker,
   study its ways and become wise.
[7]Without a chief
   or overseer or ruler,
[8]it garners its food in the summer,
   gathers its provender during harvest.
[9]How long, O slacker, will you lie there,
   when will you rise from your sleep?

[10]A little sleep, a little slumber,
   a little hugging of the arms in bed,
[11]and poverty will come upon you like a vagabond,
   destitution will come on you like a tramp.

Or, more humorously, in 22:13:

> The lazy person says, "There's a lion out there;
> on the streets I'll get killed."

Proverbs' persistent emphasis on personal free-dom, and its equating wisdom with virtue and igno-rance with malice, may make modern readers uncom-fortable. Post-Freud psychology and anthropology have amply demonstrated the complexity of human motiva-tion and the amount of unfreedom that even psychi-cally healthy people carry around with them. Personal freedom, then, is not the whole story, nor was it the whole story to the authors of Proverbs. The book is keenly aware of the givenness of human life, or "fate," and expresses it in its own style.

As a counterbalance to its emphasis on the freedom of the human agent, the book employs the concept of the "way," or the category one's action place one in. As several commentators have rightly seen, "way" is an important metaphor in Proverbs. Through one's choices a person ends up walking in "the way of the righteous" (e.g., 2:20; 4:18) or "the way of the wicked" (e.g., 4:14, 19; 12:26; 13:5,6; 15:9; 25:26). "To walk" is an age-old Near Eastern metaphor for living, for conducting oneself; it is frequent in Proverbs.[9] Proverbs frequently uses the two ways, that of the righteous and that of the wicked, in a polar contrast. Hebrew rhetoric favored such oppositions, e.g., Pharaoh vis-à-vis Yahweh in

Exodus, Lot vis-à-vis Abraham in Genesis 13-19, the nations vis-à-vis Israel generally in the Bible. To chose one path is to reject its opposite. The ways are not static, however; you may leave it, turn aside from it to the other. Each way has inherent consequences. The path is where you put yourself by your actions, and each has people walking on it. In the Proverbs' use of the two ways, one joins a community of people on the path and shares their fate.

The most extended treatment of the two ways in Proverbs is 4:10-19.

[10]Listen, my son, and take in my words
and the years of your life will be many.
[11]I point out to you the way of wisdom,
bring you to walk on the paths of justice.
[12]When you walk your step will not be thwarted
and when you run you will not stumble.
[13]Hold fast to discipline; do not let it go;
guard it, for it is life for you.
[14]Do not go on the path of the wicked!
Do not walk in the way of malefactors!
[15]Leave it! Don't go on it!
Get off it and proceed forward!
[16]For they cannot proceed until they have done evil,
they lose sleep if they do not make others stumble.
[17]They eat the bread of wickedness,
and drink the wine of violence.
[18]But the path of the righteous is like bright sunlight,
increasing in brilliance until noon.
[19]The way of the wicked is like deep darkness;
they do not know on what they stumble.

The passage adds to the metaphor of the way the images of light and darkness. The path of the righteous is lit by the brightest of light, the morning sun as it rises to its zenith in the sky; travelers on it need not worry about *unseen* perils. The word used for darkness (*ăpēlâ*) is always negative in the Bible; it is the opposite of wholesome light. It symbolizes ignorance and danger. The light-dark contrast is a harbinger of later usage, such as the children of darkness and the children of light at Qumran and in the Gospel of John.

The way is used by Sirach in the early second century B.C. (see 15:17). The doctrine of the two ways is found, much developed beyond Proverbs, in the sectarian writings at Qumran and to some extent in the Gospel of John. Qumran makes the two ways part of its ethical dualism, which it expresses as spirits created by God to struggle within human beings to dominate them until the time of God's vindication.[10] Qumran texts speak of "sons" of light or darkness, the Hebrew word *b'nê* designating groups. Dualistic terminology also appears in the New Testament, especially in John, though not implying ontological dualism: Jesus is the light shining in the darkness (1:5), he is the truth (14:26). The doctrine continues in the early Christian works, the Didache (1:1) and the Letter of Barnabas (18).

To summarize, in Proverbs' usage the way of the righteous and of the wicked functions to balance the strong emphasis on human freedom. Individuals indeed have freedom of choice but their actions have social implications. The actions place them on one of two ways, each of which has inherent consequences.

I.3. The third and most distinctive slant on moral choice in chapters 1-9 is that wisdom is a reality "out there," reified, able to be grasped. This belief is behind

Proverbs' well-known personification of wisdom as a woman.[12] Personification in the Bible is not in itself unusual, e.g., "Send forth your light and fidelity, let these be my guide" (Ps 43:3), but the extent and detail of personification in Proverbs 1-9 is without parallel in the Bible. Personification has at least three components: (a) wisdom is conceived as objective and "out there"; (b) Woman Wisdom and the other woman are persistently contrasted; (c) the world of the two women is "erotic" and "linguistic," suggesting that the stakes in the two women's rivalry are a relationship to the youth.

I.3.a. In a striking departure from extra-biblical wisdom literature, which focusses on wise acts rather than on wisdom, the word "wisdom" occurs forty-two times in Proverbs; the number is much higher if synonyms are counted.[13] Though Proverbs is concerned, like all ancient wisdom literature, with practical wisdom—knowing how to live daily life successfully and to perform one's tasks—it goes beyond the specific acts of wisdom to explore wisdom itself, its importance and limits, and its relationship to Yahweh. Given its concentration on wisdom, it is not surprising that Proverbs personifies it. Wisdom is often singled out for praise and declared to be better than all other goods: "She is more precious than corals; no treasure can compare with her" (3:15); one is urged to acquire her: "Fortunate is the person who finds [her]" (3:13) and "The beginning of wisdom: get wisdom and with all your acquisitions get insight!" (4:7). Wisdom makes one "righteous" or pleasing to God; in fact it is the essence of piety: "The beginning of wisdom is revering Yahweh, and knowledge of the Holy One is under-standing" (9:10 and see 15:33).

A further indication of the book's interest in wisdom itself is the fact that her speeches contain no specific doctrine. Instead she asks her audience to heed and not contemn her (1:20-33), to attend and to trust her words, to wait at her door as a lover (8), and to come to her banquet and live (9:1-6). Her: message is herself. The full development of this startling innovation will be in Wisdom's marriage offer, to be treated below.

I.3.b. The second element in the context of per-sonification is the persistent parallelism that the book draws between Woman Wisdom and the other woman, Seduction or Folly. As one woman speaks, the other is not far away. Woman Wisdom addresses her audience three times. The other woman is described in 2:16-19,5:1-23, and 6:30-35. She acts and speaks (though briefly) in chapter 7 and 9:13-18. Wisdom's speeches are coherent and neatly constructed; her stern first speech with its inviting final two lines (1:35) nicely balances her inviting second speech with its stern final two lines (8:36). Her banquet invitation to youths to live with her ends chapters 1-9 and looks forward to chapters10-31, especially to the final poem on the capable wife who provided her husband with a splendid household (31:10-31).[14]

Woman Folly's appearances are much more var-ied, more shaped by the genres in which they are found (such as the instructions in chapter 5 and 6:20-35 and

the example story in chapter 7), and by the require-
ments of literary contrast (such as in 2:16-19 and 9:13-
18). I suspect that the uniform portrait of Woman
Wisdom is a sign that it was created by the author of
Proverbs 1-9, *Kontrastphänomen*, to borrow a phrase
from Gustav Bostrom's 1935 monograph.[15] Woman
Wisdom has no literary antecedents that might have
served as a model to the biblical author. Some scholars,
to be sure, derive Woman Wisdom from the Egyptian
goddess Maat, but the latter is too colorless to serve as
a genuine prototype to the lively Woman Wisdom of
Proverbs; the suggestion that she is based on a Canaanite
or Phoenician goddess lacks evidence.[16]

There are, on the other hand, good antecedents to the
woman who promises life but deals death: the encounter of
the goddess Ishtar and the hero Gilgamesh in the Gilgamesh
epic of second and first-millennium Mesopotamia, the
encounter of the goddess Anat and the youth Aqhat in a
twelfth-century B.C. text, and Greek reflexes in the encounter of Circe and Calypso and Odysseus in books V and
X, respectively, of the Odyssey.

In Gilgamesh vi.1-79, the goddess Ishtar makes a
marriage proposal to Gilgamesh but he correctly per-
ceives the deadly ambivalence in her words: she is
actually inviting him to his funeral even as she offers to
be his wife.[17] Abusch has perceptively analyzed the
verbal exchange between the two:

> Ishtar offers token and substance: honor, power, and
> wealth. Here she intended to deceive Gilgamesh; she
> presented their marriage as if it were this-worldly
> whereas actually it would lead directly to his transferral

to the netherworld. Such a stratagem requires that her words admit of more than one meaning. She takes advantage of the similarities of the behavior of, and the treatment accorded to, rulers of the living and rulers of the dead. Even more important—perhaps central to the deception—are the similarities of a psychological, procedural, and symbolic nature between a wedding and a funeral. One need only recall that just as divorce may serve as a metaphor for ridding oneself of a demon and resuming a healthy state, so marriage may serve as a metaphor for demonic possession and entering into a deadly state.... In large measure these similarities derive from the fact that both marriage and death involve leaving one state and group and entering another, with the wedding and funeral facilitating the transition.[18]

The same ambivalence of life and death is present in the words of the goddess Anat to the youth Aqhat (*KTU* 1.17.vi.26-29).[19]

> Ask for life, O Aqhat the hero,
> Ask for life and I will give it to you.
> Not-dying and I will grant it to you.
> I will cause you to count years with Baal,
> With the sons of El you will count months.

When Aqhat, like Gilgamesh, refuses on the grounds that Anat does not have the power to grant life, she strikes him dead. Her words were deceptive. She offered life but dealt death, like the seductive woman in Proverbs.

I.3.c. The excerpts above highlight an important point that has escaped the notice of many: Folly's invitation is not simply to a one-time sexual liaison but to a relationship. In all the extra-biblical passages mentioned above, the goddess intends to *transform* the life of the young hero. In Gilgamesh, Ishtar will bring Gilgamesh into the underworld, i.e., she will kill him. Anat offers to confer immortality on the young man Aqhat; she will eventually killing him. Calypso keeps Odysseus from returning to his old life, and Circe wants to turn him into a pig. The seductive woman in Proverbs likewise intends to change the young man. Though promising life, she will kill him (2:16-18; 5:5; 7:23-27; 9:17-18).

Wisdom, the literary "contrast-phenomenon" of Folly, also wants to change the life of her faithful adherents. She offers them a relationship. The extraordinary consequences of their invitations is why both women's words are considered so important. Are their words trustworthy? Is it true or false life they are offering? Woman Folly is described as speaking words that deal death (2:16-19; 5:3-6; 6:24-26; 7; 9:17-18). Woman Wisdom, on the other hand, speaks "straight," she is "on the level." Her words set up a relationship between herself and her hearer, and she herself becomes the message: if you spurn me, I will leave you to your own devices (1:20-33), if you listen to me and wait at my door, you will find life and favor from the Lord (chapters 8 and 9). Woman Wisdom, in short, offers herself to the youth.

The traditional titles for personified Wisdom— Dame Wisdom; or Lady Wisdom—are seriously misleading. "Dame" and "Lady" imply that she is matronly, and that she will be a mother or a patron to the youth. This is not true. She should be called Woman

Wisdom, for her appeal to the youth is erotic, as Roland Murphy has pointed out. The young man is urged to "find" her (3:13; 8:17, 35) as one "finds" a good wife (18:22; 31:10). The language of "seeking and finding" her (8:17) comes from love poetry such as Cant 3:1 and 5:6. The young man is told to love and embrace Wisdom (Prov 4:6-8) and call her "my sister" (7:4), which is the title given to the beloved in Cant 4:9-5:1. "Those who love me I also love," she promises (8:17). And like the Song of Songs (2:9; 5:4), her love must "watch daily at her gates, wait at her doorpost" (8:34).[20]

We are now in a position to appreciate the great analogy of Proverbs 1-9 between finding a wife and finding wisdom. The original historical and social context was that of a young man leaving his parental house (1:8-19) to establish his own house. Building a household implies finding a wife, establishing a basic relationship for one's life. One must be faithful to one's wife (5:15-19) lest one lose one's property (5:10; 6:30-31), one's vigor (5:9; 6:32-33), one' reputation (5:14), one's very life (2:18-19; 5:22-23; 7:23; 9:17-18). And so with Woman Wisdom. You must choose her, trust her, and be ever-faithful. As fidelity to one's spouse is achieved by rejecting others' allurements, so Wisdom is acquired by rejecting foolish and wicked behavior. The other woman is "foreign" or "strange," i.e., out of place, the wrong one, out of bounds for marriage.[21]

The most important poem on the relationship of the disciple to Wisdom in Proverbs is chapter 8. As already noted, the speech is parallel to Wisdom's stern opening address in 1:20-33. It also artfully reverses the extraordinary night seduction of the "simple" youth in chapter 7. The scenario in chapter 8 is not, as in chapter 7, a lone youth, night, the adulteress's house, but their opposite: a crowd of people, broad daylight, the city gates where public business was conducted. Her speech in vv. 4-10 gives no special teaching but is an appeal for trust and esteem:

"To you I call,
    raise my voice to the sons of men."
[5]Learn shrewdness, O simple ones,
    ready your heart, O foolish ones.
[6]Listen, for I will speak noble words,
    open my lips with the right words;
[7]what my mouth utters is worthy of trust;
    malicious talk is abhorrent to my lips.
[8]In righteousness (are spoken) all the words of my mouth,
    none of them are twisted or perverted.
[9]All of them are plain to the intelligent person,
    straight to those who have attained knowledge.

In the second part of her address (vv. 12-21), she reveals why her words are worthy of trust—she dwells with prudence, rejects lies, is the source of royal wisdom, gives gifts to her lovers.

The third section of chapter 8, w. 22-31, the famous passage on Wisdom's role in creation, provides the ultimate grounding of her authority.

[22]Yahweh begot me at the beginning of his rule,
    the first of his deeds long ago.
[23]Of old I was formed,
    at the beginning, prior to the earth.

"Temporal" priority is a mark of honor and affection. Similarly honoring Wisdom are the chiastically ar-

ranged phrases, "I was there...//I was beside him.[22]
Then comes a most revealing couplet:

I was (his) *delight* daily,
    playing before him at all times,
[31]*playing* in his inhabited world;
    my *delight* is to be with the human race.

The text draws an analogy between delighting in and
playing with Yahweh in heaven and in delighting and
playing with human beings on earth. The words have
an erotic or, more accurately, marital meaning. Note
what is *not* said in this poem, whose purpose is to
establish Woman Wisdom's authority: I saw how God
made the world because I was there and so I can let you
in on its secrets. What is said rather is: I am Yahweh's
beloved, the object of his love and esteem, and thus I can
be your beloved or lover. Wisdom's authority, then, is
not that she can bestow the secrets of the universe but
that she is Yahweh's beloved. And she desires a like
relation with human beings:

[32]And now, O sons, listen to me:
[33]discipline and wisdom do not spurn.
Happy those who keep my ways,
    and happy the person who heeds me,
[34]who watches daily at my gates,
    attending at the doorpost of my gates.
[35]For whoever finds me finds life,
    and gains the favor from Yahweh.[23]

With this speech Wisdom reveals herself except for one
thing. In chapter 9 Wisdom invites the youth into her
house.

[1]Wisdom has built her house,
    has hewn seven pillars.
[2]She has slaughtered her meat, poured her wine,

Yes, she has set her table.
³She sends out her maidservants,
she calls on the top of the heights of the city:
⁴"Whoever is simple, let him come in here,
(whoever) lacks sense, I say (LXX) to him (lit. you),
⁵Come, eat of my food,
and drink the wine I have poured.
⁶Leave simplicity (LXX) behind and live,
walk on the road of discernment.

Wisdom celebrates the building of her house with a feast. Instead of inviting the denizens of heaven, where she lives (8:27a, 30a), she invites human beings, "Whoever is simple...lacking knowledge..." to "abandon simplicity [G] and live...walk in the way of insight" (vv. 4-6).

What is the life she offers? According to the text, it is the opposite of living in "simplicity" or ignorance. To live most probably means to live *with* Wisdom, to banquet with her in her house. As in other passages in the Bible (e.g. Genesis 2-3; Ps 27:4: 84:4), it does not mean mere biological life but life with another.

Chapter 9 ends the first major section of the book (chapters 1-9) and looks forward to the individual sayings in chapters 10-31. Chapters 1-9 have helped readers re-imagine morality. The chapters teach that wisdom herself is more important than any single wise action. The disciple must first desire her and pursue her over any good. She lies within their grasp. Chapters 8 and 9 have promised that the disciple can live in Wisdom's house. The following chapters will suggest that living with her will be partly through pondering the sayings in chapters 10-31. We will see that most of the sayings are not immediately obvious, that they challenge the reader to read and think, i.e., to practice discernment. Living in Wisdom's house is as challenging and rewarding as living with one's spouse.

PART II

Chapters 10 to 31 consist mostly of two-line sayings, though there are a few instructions and exhortations. This part of Proverbs has been somewhat neglected by readers, apart from a few famous proverbs such as "Pride goeth before destruction, and an r haughty spirit before a fall" (16:18); "spare the rod and spoil the child" (not found in Proverbs in those exact words)[24] and soft answer turneth away wrath" (15:1).

I believe that the sayings are a school of discernment, meant for people who want to direct their lives in wisdom and to live in Wisdom's house. Life, according to Proverbs, is not to be lived without reflection, for there is more than at first appears. This is why the sayings are important; they teach the disciple to reflect on ordinary-looking statements and thus to reflect on ordinary life.

Before looking at these sayings, however, we should note the remarkable emphasis on knowing in Proverbs. It reminds one of the intellectuality of later Jewish sages, who are also called "wise," or of medieval scholasticism, which put a premium on knowledge for its own sake. Synonyms of knowing pile up in Proverbs, each with its own nuance but, used cumulatively, signifying virtually the same thing. Why this enormous emphasis on knowing? In answering, one should not adopt the feeling-thought dichotomy of modern epistemology nor the sharp speculative-practical distinction of popular culture. The simplest explanation, perhaps, is that the wisdom in Proverbs is closest to our *discernment*, the ability to perceive a reality or situation aright, under the three related aspects of sapiential, ethical, and religious, a trio noted by Alonso-Schökel in his commentary on Proverbs.

Let us now look at the sayings, that we too might "practice wisdom." To study them and wrestle with their meaning is to live with Wisdom. The first proverb in the first Solomonic collection (10:1-22:16) is:

A wise son makes his father rejoice,
  but a foolish son is a grief to his mother.

Incidentally, but not unimportantly, this and like sayings presupposing males pose a serious problem to English translators.

For example, the *NRSV* renders:

A wise child makes a glad father,
  but a foolish child is a mother's grief.

The rendering is adequate except for the word "child" used as a gender-neutral term for Hebrew *ben*, "son." "Child" is the wrong word, for it means a person *incapable* of making publicly recognized decisions, whereas the person addressed by Proverbs is precisely capable of such decisions. That's what the book is about! In my judgment, the two best English translations of Proverbs are the Jewish Publication Society version (sometimes called the New Jewish Version) and the New American Bible. Both are sensitive to the wit and wordplay.

Back to our saying. The aphorism linking offspring's wisdom to parental emotion is not so banal as it at first seems. Wisdom in the book is not speculative knowledge but knowledge about life along with skill to act. Parents' feelings about their children's wisdom in the sense of living well will be much different than their feelings about their children's wisdom in the sense of graduate school knowledge. The young person in Proverbs represents the family to the community and the person's success in living entails consequences so serious that can be termed life or death.

Simple but deft artistry underlines the meaning of this saying. The exteriority of the father's response (verbs of emotion often imply expression of the emotion) is contrasted with the interiority of the mother's response (*tûgâ*) means inner grief).[25] Note the two-line or bi-colon form, which is characteristic of Hebrew poetry. The first line is repeated in the second line; it is expanded or altered in a negative or positive direction. The reader pauses at the threshold of the second line wondering: Where it will go? In this saying, line B can go in a number of directions. The nine or so variants of the saying in subsequent chapters show us some of the possibilities (13:1; 15:20; 17:25; 19:13; 19:26; 23:15, 22-25; 27:11; 29:15). In 15:20, the B line is, "but a foolish son shames his mother." Instead of the contrast of 10:1 between inner maternal grief and extrovert paternal joy, the contrast is between public celebration and public shame. Another variant is 13:1:

A wise son? Credit the discipline of the father;
  a scoffer will not listen to rebuke.

Wise offspring are a tribute to their parents (who took the time to give them training) as well as to themselves (who were willing to receive it). These varied sayings about the effect on the parent of the *petî*, the untaught, provide a thread through the whole book.

Sayings in Proverbs are generally less obvious than most English proverbs, which have to establish their authority quickly. The hearer must get their point immediately. Compare "Fools walk in where angels fear to tread," with 22:3, "The shrewd person sees trouble and withdraws, but the naive keep on going and pay the penalty." or "Waste not want not" with 11:24, "One person gives freely yet acquires more, while another, keeping even what is owed, grows poorer."

That most biblical proverbs yield their meaning only to probing hearers suggests their authors' intent is to reveal by concealing. The long-time reader of Proverbs becomes suspicious if the saying yields its meaning immediately.

Truthful lips abide forever,
  but a lying tongue only for a moment (12:19).

The saying has a double meaning: (1) lies are quickly found out whereas truth lasts; (2) truth tellers, favored by God, live long. As often, the source organ stands for its "product": eyes and tongue stands for words. 14:4:

Where there are no oxen, the crib is clean,
  but bountiful crops come from the strength of the ox.

If one has no animals, one does not have the burden of keeping the crib full, but without them one will have no crops to fill the barn. You don't get something for nothing. The reversal of line A in line B is supported by the reversal of *bar*, "clean," in *rab*, "bountiful." Another saying requiring a second or third reading is 14:28:

> In a multitude of people is the glory of a king,
>> but when the people become few—kingship fares ill.

In stating that the more numerous the people the more worthy of respect is their king, the saying subjects kingship to critique: a king's glory depends not on himself but on his people, and it is dangerous for him if his people are too few. 14:33:

> Wisdom can remain silent in the midst of the wise,
>> but amid fools it must make itself known.

The Greek translation of the second century B.C. (followed by the Syriac several centuries later) added "not" in the first line: "Wisdom *cannot* be silent in the midst of the wise." The versions failed to appreciate the nuance of Hebrew *tānûah*, "to rest, remain silent." The point is that wisdom can rest content, need not speak out, among the wise, but it cannot remain silent among fools. The Hebrew prepositions in each cola can mean both "in the heart of, within" (e.g., Jer 31:33) or "in the midst of, amid" (e.g., Exod 15:3; Amos 7:8). A nice example of the role of "discipline" (*mûsar*) in the education of a wise person is 19:25:

> Beat a scoffer and even the simple become wise;
>> merely correct an intelligent person and he will understand.

The contrasts are striking—to beat, to rebuke; the incapacity of the scoffer to learn even from blows; the quickness of the intelligent person to learn from the slightest gesture. The latter point is wittily made: even a naive youth learns the lesson the scoffer cannot. Words are enormously important in Proverbs. 18:20:

> From the fruit of a person's mouth his belly is filled;
> with the produce of his lips he is sated.

"Mouth" and "lips" are a fixed noun pair. The saying trades on the commonplace that people reap what they sow, e.g., "[the rebellious] shall eat the fruit of their ways, be sated with their own plans" (1:33). Here convictions about the importance of language trans-form the commonplace: the inward attitude and out-ward expression symbolized by one's words determine one's destiny. The saying plays on the expectation that hunger is sated by what comes through the mouth.

Some sayings engage the reader by their wit and, occasionally, by their humor, albeit of a sardonic kind, as in 27:14:

> Whoever greets his neighbor with a loud voice early in the morning,
> it will be reckoned to him as a curse.

Hebrew *bērēk* means both "to greet" and "to bless," i.e., whoever "blesses" his neighbor...will come back on his head as a curse."[26] 12:11:

> Whoever tills his field will have plenty of food,
> but whoever pursues vanity will have a lack of mind.

The contrast is between steadily working one's fields and energetically chasing illusions, and between sur-plus and lack. 14:3:

> In the mouth of a fool is a twig of pride,
> but the lips of the wise provide protection for them.

Mouth (or tongue) and lips are often paired in Proverbs as in 10:32; 16:10; 18:6, 20; 27:2. The organ stands for what it produces—words. "Twig" as a term for tongue is perhaps a play on the tongue as a powerful instrument of protection, like the sword-tongue of Ps 57:5; 59:8; and Prov 5:4. Sages' words protect them whereas fools' tongues get them into trouble. Another bit of humor appears in 14:29, where the Hebrew idioms retain much of their meaning in English:

To be long on patience is to be great in wisdom,
    to be short in temper is to heighten folly.

A final example of sardonic humor (and of attitudes toward child rearing) is 23:12:

Do not withhold discipline from a youth.
    If you strike him with a rod he will not die.
Strike him with a rod
    and you will save his soul from Sheol.

The exhortation plays humorously on death: the young person will not die from instructional blows but from their absence, for premature death will result from uncorrected folly. It should be said that this harsh command is followed immediately by a tender sentiment: "My son, if your heart becomes wise, my heart will rejoice, yes mine."

Where is Yahweh, the God of Israel, in the sayings? Some scholars have made the case that "old wisdom" was secular and only later did God-language and "other items of vocabulary expressive of a moralism which derives from Yahwistic piety"[27] come to be added. Most scholars remain unpersuaded by supposed "Yahwehizing," for Egyptian and Mesopotamian wisdom literature were thoroughly religious from their origins,[29] and the assumptions upon which the reconstruction rests are questionable. The following sayings about Yahweh,

therefore, cannot be dated late just because they mention the divine name. 16:1:

The designs of the heart belong to a human being,
but from Yahweh is the answer of the tongue.

There are several oppositions, as is often the case with
the proverbs: human being/God, heart/tongue, designs (plural)/answer (singular), "belong to"/"from."
Interpretation of this enigmatic saying have ranged
from "Man proposes but God disposes" to Delitzsch's
view that God's answer is in the moment of expression.
An important clue, in my opinion, is the frequent
contrast in Proverbs between heart and tongue (or
mouth or lips): the pairing expresses the full process of
deciding and doing. A person may dream of projects
but the power to realize them is not within human
power. 16:2:

All the ways of an individual are pure in his own eyes,
but Yahweh searches spirits.

"Pure" is a moral word in Job and Proverbs. Self-
assessments are incomplete and tentative, subject to the
judgment of Yahweh. 20:30:

There is no wisdom, there is no discernment,
there is no knowledge that can prevail against Yahweh.

It is a striking way of stating that Yahweh is the source
of all wisdom. The paradox is that wisdom prevails
except against its source, Yahweh. 22:2:

A rich person meets a poor person;
Yahweh made them both.

Poor and rich people come into contact in a variety of
ways and their relationship is ordinarily dictated by
considerations of wealth. Line B relativizes such dis-

tinctions by naming Yahweh the creator and sustainer
of every human being. 14:19:

> The malicious will sink down in the presence of the good,
> and the wicked, before the gates of the righteous.

There are evidently two meanings: (1) the wicked are
put down as in 1 Sam 2:7 ("[Yahweh] casts down, he
also lifts high"); (2) the wicked will bow down before
the good as their superiors. For a New Testament
application, see Luke 16:19-21, the story of Lazarus,
"And at [the rich man's] gate lay a poor person named
Lazarus."

The statement is sometimes made that the Book of
Proverbs is only interested in ensuring a successful
human life. It is said that one ascertains the way things
are, the "order" over which God presides, and then
determines the order of retribution. Good conduct
brings wealth and prosperity and evil conduct incurs
punishment. This viewpoint, it is alleged, is later
subject to severe challenge by the honest and searching
books of Qoheleth and Job.[30] The best response to the
assertion is to look at what some form critics call
"observations," i.e., sayings that are not didactic but
simply "tell it the way it is."[31] A good example is 20:14:

> 'Bad! Bad!' says the purchaser,
> then goes off and boasts.

Actually, this is a bit more than a pure observation, since
it says something about convention in language and the
need to assess words in their context. In observations
Proverbs often handles the problem of justice, which in
the wisdom literature was often posed as the prosperity

of the wicked person or, more rarely, the suffering of
the innocent as with Job. Many of the sayings about
wealth fall here.[32] 10:15:

> The resources of the wealthy is their mighty city,
>   the ruin of the poor is their poverty.

The saying is a neutral observation: their wealth pro-
tects the rich whereas their lack of resources is disastrous
for the poor. Similar is 18:23:

> The poor person must say "please,"
>   but the wealthy man speaks abruptly.

Like other observations about poverty (10:15; 13:7, 8,
23; 14:20; 19:4, 7; 22:7; 28:15), this one simply states
the situation of the poor person (but not their degra-
dation). 13:7-8 make similar observations.

> There are people who act rich but have nothing;
>   others act poor but have great wealth.
> His great wealth is ransom for a rich person,
>   but the poor person never even hears a shout.

Vv. 7-8 both concern riches and poverty and comment
on each other. V. 7 suggests, like 12:9, that possessions
do not always reveal the true state of a person. V. 8
continues the critique of wealth by suggesting at once
its value—it can save the wealthy person's life by the
payment of ransom, but a poor person is in a sense
protected by not having possessions and never experiences the cry of the pursuer (like the use of *ge'ārâ* in Isa
30:17, "A thousand shall flee at the cry of one"). The
ordinary meaning of "hearing rebuke," which is the
mark of the wise (v. 1 and Qoh 7:5) would not parallel
line A, though that is how the versions take it. 14:20:

> Even by his companions the poor person is shunned,
>   but the friends of a rich person are many.

This is an unsparing observation on the connection between wealth and esteem. Related is 18:24:

> There are friends who spend time with you,
>> and there is a friend who clings closer than kin.

This observation records the fact that most friends are good for company but not for trouble.

Didactic sayings, especially the "better than" ones that assign relative values, provide further evidence that Proverbs does not ordinarily measure people by money. 15:16-17:

> Better a little with fear of Yahweh,
>> than great treasure accompanied by confusion.
> Better a portion of vegetables where love is,
>> than a stall-fed ox where hatred is.

The book occasionally calls into question what it ordinarily sets a high value on—words. 26:4-5:

> Do not answer a fool according to his folly,
>> lest you yourself become like him.
> Answer a fool according to his folly,
>> lest he become wise in his own eyes.

One can hardly find a clearer statement that a proverb depends on its context for its truth. Recall the definition of a proverb by Wolfgang Mieder: a concise statement of an *apparent* truth having currency. "Apparent" allows context to play a role.

Several more sayings underscore the limits of human knowledge and discernment. 20:11:

> Even a child may dissemble in its actions,
>> though its actions be pure and upright.

The saying seems to be about the inscrutability of the human heart, like 13:7 and 14:13. One cannot infallibly read it from outward behavior, for even children know how to play-act. 21:8:

> Twisted may be the path of a person, and unfamiliar,
> but his actions are blameless and right.

Though most translations make a simple opposition between wicked and good behavior (e.g., Plöger, "Twisted is the way of a guilty person, but the pure— upright is his action") the adjectives describing the way in line A are morally neutral ("winding" is unique in the Bible), not "perverse." The vocabulary of line B is identical to 20:11b, which denies intentions can infallibly be read off external actions.

Another way in which Proverbs shows its own perspective is its adapting of Egyptian wisdom literature. Soon after the publication in 1923 of the Egyptian Instruction of Amenemope of the thirteenth century B.C., scholars concluded that Proverbs 22:17-24:22 was modeled upon it. The Egyptian work has thirty chapters which correspond to the thirty units of Proverbs 22:17-24:22; there are also close thematic and verbal similarities. The Israelite adaptation shows not only wit and skill but also a characteristic concern with wisdom in itself. One section, 22:29-23:9 (framed by the mention of boundary markers) seems to be a self-conscious reflection on the sage's vocation. It begins with a strong affirmation that a sage's *wisdom* will assure his career (22:29): "Do you see a person skilled in his craft? He will enter the service of kings, he will not enter the service of the obscure." The immediately following section indirectly supports the vocation of a sage by

warning against advancing oneself through means other
than wisdom—dining with rulers (23:1-3), pursuing
wealth (23:4-5), forcing oneself on unwilling hosts
(23:6-8), or displaying one's erudition (23:9). 23:1-3 is
worth looking at for its double meaning.

> When you sit down to dine with a ruler,
>> consider carefully what is before you;
> And stick the knife in your jaw
>> if you have a big appetite.
> Do not desire his viands,
>> for it is a food that deceives.

Dining etiquette is found in two Old Kingdom instructions as well as in Amenemope (chaps. 23 and 26).
Luxurious meals apparently were rare enough to be
occasions of intemperance and of subsequent regret.
Amenemope chapter 26 (XXIV.2-XXX.15) warns against
using a repast to curry favor with one's social betters
("Do not sit down in the beer house / in order to join
one greater than you."). Chapter 23 is especially rel-
evant to our passage: "Do not eat in the presence of an
official / And then set your mouth before <him>; / If
you are sated pretend to chew, / Content yourself with
your saliva. / Look at the bowl that is before you, / And
let it serve your needs." (XXIII.13-20). Our passage goes
beyond table etiquette to expose the folly of the social
ploy itself. Crucial is the *double entendre* "set before
you," which refers both to food and host: Consider
carefully the food/host before you and put your knife
not to your food to satisfy your hunger but to your over-
eager jaws. If you don't, you will obtain neither food nor
favor.

The usual scholarly interpretation—a sage should show modesty and restraint at the meals of the powerful—does not fit the language. First, the Hebrew idiom in v. 1b, "understand completely, consider carefully," is inappropriate for food alone. Second, sticking one's table knife in oneself rather than in one's food at the moment of greatest hunger shows that the entire business of currying favor is ridiculous. Incidentally, the *NAB* and *NRSV* translation, "Put a knife to your throat," (lit. "Stick the knife in your jaw") is misleading because it uses an English idiom for threatening with death. Third, "food that deceives" in v. 3a is best read on the two levels already established: the meal that cannot be eaten because of the need to restrain oneself and the meal that cannot further one's career.

Another excerpt from the same "Words of the Wise" is a satiric portrait of a drunkard, which may also be based on Egyptian models. The Egyptian Instruction of Any, written between 1500-1300 B.C., has similarities to Prov 23:29-35: "Don't indulge in drinking beer, / Lest you utter evil speech / And don't know what you're saying. / If you fall and hurt your body, / None holds out a hand to you: / Your companions in the drinking / Stand up saying: "Out with the drunk!" / If one comes to seek you and talk with you, / One finds you lying on the ground, / As if you were a little child."[33]

[31]Do not gaze at wine because it is red,
  because it sparkles in the cup,
  goes down smoothly.
[32]Afterwards it bites like a snake,
  stings like a viper.

³³Your eyes will see strange sights,
   your heart will give voice to absurdities.
³⁴And you will be like someone sleeping in mid-ocean,
   like someone sleeping on the top of a mast.
³⁵"They beat me up but I'm not hurt,
   they clubbed me but I didn't feel it.
When can I wake up,
   can I go out and look for more?"

As in the portrait of the naive youth in 7:6-23, v. 31 catches the fascination with imagined pleasures. The anticipated pleasures of alcohol turn out to be the bite of a snake—hallucinations, vertigo, and blackout. Such physical horrors teach fools nothing (v. 35cd), for by definition they cannot learn from "rebuke," i.e., hard knocks. For the sensations of the drink, the poet uses vivid images: the bite of a snake, the sway and seasickness of a sailor.

Before leaving the sayings of Proverbs we must look at one extended comparison. In Roland Murphy's excellent little book *Responses to 101 Questions on the Psalms and Other Writings*³⁴ he is asked, "What is your favorite proverb?" His choice is 30:18-19, for which he gives a fine explanation.

   Three things are too wonderful for me,
      yes, four I cannot understand:
   The way of an eagle in the air,
      the way of a serpent on a rock,
   The way of a ship on the sea,
      and the way of a man with a maiden.

Murphy remarks:

   The key to the saying lies in the fourfold repetition of the word, "way." The way in each case is purposeful, but its path is difficult to follow or control…. The climax comes in the fourth example: the mystery of the attraction between a man and a woman—the path that brings them together, and with such fateful consequences. This "way" embraces a mysterious providence at which the sage marvels. The mysteries of nature serve to enhance the total longing which attracts and binds men and women together. In Genesis 3:16 we read that the desire of the woman is for the man, and in Canticles 7:11 that the man's desire is for the woman.[35]

In summary, part II tells us that to study the wise sayings is to walk with Wisdom and to live in her house. They help the disciple to practice the art of discernment and find wisdom in the world. As one considers the ordinary-seeming sayings to get their meaning, so does one learn to understand ordinary life.

PART III

The final section is concerned with the Book of Proverbs as a book within the Christian Bible. I believe the question should be posed as the place of the book within the entire biblical library rather than the relationship of Proverbs to the New Testament. The Bible is a library as well as two testaments or covenants. The canon is not simply an archive; its books relate to each other in a lively dialectic. Some books, it is true, have little to say to each other, but others are in vigorous dialogue, e.g., Deuteronomy and Exodus, the gospels of Mark and John. Proverbs has little to do directly with the great historical and legal works of the Bible (the Pentateuch and the Deuteronomistic History) and with the prophets. It says nothing explicit about the

history of Israel, never mentions the central institutions
of covenant and law, and passes over in silence the great
leaders Moses and David. It is nonetheless not at the
margins of the Bible, for it stands within a venerable
Near Eastern gnomic and instructional tradition that
includes the Old Testament books of Job, Qoheleth,
Sirach, and the Book of Wisdom. The relationship of
Job and Qoheleth to Proverbs should not be overstated,
as they sometimes are. To interpret Job and Qoheleth
as direct responses to Proverbs relies too much on a
"history of ideas" approach and slights the proper aims
of Job and Qoheleth. The Book of Sirach in the early
second century B.C. is a different matter. It regards
Proverbs as a sacred book, expanding and popularizing
some of its main ideas just as it does with the Pentateuch
and the prophets.

How does Proverbs relate to the books of the New
Testament? Do its emphases on wisdom as the great
quest of the disciple and on sayings as exercises in
discernment continue among early Christians? The
answer to the first question is an emphatic yes. Early
Christians saw Jesus as incarnate wisdom. Of all the
writings, the Gospel of John most persistently regards
Jesus as incarnate wisdom descended from on high to
offer human beings life and truth. The Gospel expresses
Jesus' heavenly origin by identifying him with personified Wisdom. Woman Wisdom was with God from
the beginning, even before the earth (Prov 8:22-23),

[22]Yahweh begot me at the beginning of his rule,
     the first of his deeds long ago.

[23]Of old I was formed,
  at the beginning, prior to the earth.
[24]When he established the heavens, I was there.

Jesus is the Word in the beginning (John 1:1, "In the beginning was the Word, and the Word was with God), with the Father before the world existed (John 17:5, "the glory that I had with you before the world began"). Wisdom shows human beings how to walk in the way that leads to life (Prov 2:20-22, "*so that* you may walk on the way of the good") 36 and Jesus functions as revealer in John. He speaks in long discourses like Woman Wisdom in Prov 1:20-33 and chapter 8. Wisdom invites people to partake of her rich banquet, where the food and drink symbolize life and closeness to God (Prov 9:2-5), and Jesus does the same: "I am the bread of life. Whoever comes to me will never be hungry and whoever believes in me will never be thirsty" (John 6:35). Wisdom seeks friends (Prov 1:30-31, "But the person who listens to me dwells secure, is at rest, free from the fear of trouble), so Jesus recruits followers (John 1:36-38, 43 "Come and you will see.... Come, follow me"). The possibility exists of rejecting Wisdom (Prov 1:24-25) and also Jesus (John 8:46; 10:25). Elsewhere in the New Testament, Col 1:15-20 applies to Christ ideas of pre-existence and creativity taken from Prov 8:22-31.

Did the sayings of Proverbs exercise influence on New Testament writings? As is today widely recognized, sometimes to an exaggerated degree, Jesus himself was a sage and teacher. He taught in ways that involved his hearers, especially in the parables. New Testament parables seem to do what sayings do in Proverbs—invite the hearer to look at life afresh through pondering the parable. One memorable instance of his employing aphorisms and appreciating the response of others to them is Matthew 15:21-28, the incident of the Syro-Phoenician woman. The encounter between Jesus and the woman reminds one of two peasants hurling proverbs at each other.

> He said in reply [to his disciples], "I was sent only to the house of Israel." But the woman came and did him homage, saying, "Lord, help me." He said in replay, "It is not right to take the food of the children and throw it to the dogs." She said, "Please, Lord, for even the dogs eat the scraps that fall from the table of their masters." Then Jesus said to her in reply, "O woman, great is your faith! Let it be done for you as you wish." And her daughter was healed from that hour.

One is tempted to comment that it was not only her great faith that won Jesus over but her considerable wit.

The great repository of sayings in the New Testament writings is the Letter of James. Though classed among the seven catholic *epistles*, it is a letter only by its opening address, "James the servant of God and of the Lord Jesus Christ, to the twelve tribes in the dispersion, greetings" (1:1). The work is a series of instructions using the familiar exhortatory verbs followed by motives, often in the form of sayings or proverbs. Old wisdom themes appear: the danger of an unbridled tongue in chapter 3 (cf. Prov 10:18-21), of presumptuous planning in 4:13-17 (cf. Prov 16:1), of ill-gotten wealth 5:1-6 (cf. Prov 10:2-3). Though commonsensical in the style of the instruction, James nonetheless exalts "wisdom from above" (3:13-18 and cf. 1:17), continuing the Old Testament tradition of wisdom beyond human capacity but graciously given to human beings by God (Proverbs 2; 8; Job 28; Sirach 24). James' wisdom instruction does not continue the old material unchanged, however, for it introduces denunciations of the callous rich from the prophets (1:27; 2:1 13; 4:1-10; 5:1-6).

In summary, the Book of Proverbs is a resource for people today. Within the framework of belief in the God of Israel, it is both a visionary writing and a practical manual. It proposes that wisdom is an ever-present horizon in moral choice and that the disciple should recognize, love, and pursue it prior to any concern with individual actions. The many sayings in the book are like goads (Qoh 12:11), training the disciple in discernment, the capacity to see and act aright in ordinary life. Proverbs exhorts the disciple to a lifelong search for the wisdom inherent in all noble activity. Such a search, carried out in love and linked to other basic quests, ultimately puts one in touch with God. Further, the book upholds reverence for teachers and their instruction as a way to wisdom without identifying wisdom with a particular teacher or instruction. It links the sapiential, ethical, and religious dimension of human existence in a new way.

NOTES

1. Despite the relative lack of popular interest, there has been an increase of scholarly interest in recent years. Recent surveys of scholarly literature include J. J. Burden, "The Wisdom of Many: Recent Changes in Old Testament Proverb Interpretation," *Old Testament Essays* 3 (1990) 341-59; H. Delkurt, "Grundprobleme alttestamentlicher Weisheit," *Verkündigung und Forschung* 36 (1991) 38-69; R. Murphy, "Recent Research on Proverbs and Qoheleth," *Currents in Research* 1 (1993) 119-40.

2. Indispensable for the question of the unity of Proverbs is P. W. Skehan, "A Single Editor for the Whole Book of Proverbs," The *Catholic Biblical Quarterly* 10 (1948) 115-130; a revised version appears in Skehan, *Studies in Israelite Poetry and Wisdom* (The Catholic Biblical Quarterly Monograph Series 1; Washington: Catholic Biblical Association, 1971).

3. R. Wolkomir, "A proverb each day keeps this scholar at play," *Smithsonian* (Sept. 1992) 112. Few of the sayings in Proverbs had currency among the people, so they are not proverbs in a technical sense.

4. Some paremiologists such as Archer Taylor believe a proverb cannot be defined: "The definition of a proverb is too difficult to repay the undertaking.... An incommunicable quality tells us this sentence is proverbial and that one is not.... Let us be content with recognizing that a proverb is a saying current among the folk," in *The Proverb and an Index to the Proverb* (2nd ed.; Copenhagen and Hatboro: Rosenkilde & Baggers, 1962) 3.

5. Gerhard von Rad, *Wisdom in Israel* (Nashville: Abingdon, 1972), underscores the thetic character of wisdom literature.

6. "The Pedagogy of Proverbs 2," *Journal of Biblical Literature* 113 (1994) 243. Italics his.

7. For a detailed study of Proverbs' vocabulary of wisdom, see M. Fox, "Words for Wisdom," *Zeitschrift für Althebraistik* 6 (1993) 149-65.

8. N. Habel, "The Symbolism of Wisdom in Proverbs 1-9," *Interpretation* 26 (1972) 131-57 and R. C. Van Leeuwen, "Liminality and Worldview in Proverbs 1-9," *Semeia* 50 (1990) 111-44.

9. F. J. Helfmeyer, "Halakh," *Theological Dictionary of the Old Testament* (ed. G. J. Botterweck and H. Ringgren; Grand Rapids: Eerdmans, 1978) 388-403.

10. A handy summary of Qumran and Johannine usage may be found in J. A. Fitzmyer, *Responses to 101 Questions on the Dead Sea Scrolls* (New York: Paulist, 1992) 122-25.

11. For a review of some of the evidence (exclusive of Proverbs) see S. Brock, "The Two Ways and the Palestinian Targum," in A Tribute to Geza Vermes: Essays on Jewish and Christian Literature *and History* (P. R. Davies and R. T. White, eds.; *Journal for the Study of the Old Testament* 100; Sheffield: Sheffield Academic Press, 1990) 139-52.

12. For a good review of the setting of personification in Proverbs, see R. Murphy, *The Tree of Life: An Exploration of Biblical Wisdom Literature* (Anchor Bible Reference Library; New York: Doubleday, 1990) 17-18, 133-49. Basic to the modern discussion is G. von Rad, "The Self-Revelation of Creation," in his *Wisdom in Israel* (Nashville: Abingdon, 1972) 144-76.

13. The concern holds good for other biblical wisdom books: 18 times in Job, 28 times in Qoheleth, 60 times (Greek *sophia*) in Sirach, and 30 times in the Wisdom of Solomon.

14. For a recent statement of this view, see T. McCreesh, "Wisdom as Wife: Proverbs 31:10-31," *Revue Biblique* 92 (1985) 25-46.

15. Chapter seven is an "example story" like 24:33-34. See R. Murphy *Wisdom Literature* (Forms of Old Testament Literature 13; Grand Rapids: Eerdmans, 1981) 76.

16. Further, see R. Clifford, "Woman Wisdom in the Book of Proverbs," in *Biblische Theologie und gesellschaftlicher Wandel* (Lohfink volume; Freiburg: Herder, 1992) 61-72.

17. T. Abusch, "Ishtar's Proposal and Gilgamesh's Refusal: An Interpretation of *The Gilgamesh Epic,* Tablet 6, Lines 1-79," *History of Religions* 26 (1986-87) 160-61.

18. Abusch, "Ishtar's Proposal," 157-58.

19. KTU = *The keilalphabetischen Texte aus Ugarit* (ed. M. Dietrich, O. Loretz, J. Sanmartin; Neukirchen-Vluyn: Neukirchener Verlag, 1976), which is the most complete transcription of the Ugaritic texts.

20. "Wisdom and Eros in Proverbs 1-9," *The Catholic Biblical Quarterly* 50 (1988) 600-03.

21. Harold Washington, "The Strange Woman (*'šh zrh/ nkryh*) of Proverbs 1-9 and Post-Exilic Judaean Society," in *Second Temple Studies* (T. C. Eskenazi and K. H. Richards, eds.; Sheffield: Sheffield Academic Press, 1994) 217-42.

22. For the chiasm, G. Yee, "The Theology of Creation in Proverbs 8:22-31," in *Creation in the Biblical Traditions* (Catholic Biblical Monograph Series 24; Washington: Catholic Biblical Association, 1992) 88.

23. I follow the *New American Bible,* which depends on the Septuagint here.

24. Versions are found in 13:24; 19:18; 22:15; 23:13; 19:15, 17.

25. Its three occurrences in Ps 119:23; Prov 14:13; 17:21 imply inner anguish.

26. As noted in *Notes on the New Translation of The Torah* (ed. H. Orlinsky; Philadelphia: Jewish Publication Society, 1970) 115.

27. E.g., W. McKane, *Proverbs A New Approach* (Old Testament Library; Philadelphia: Westminster, 1970) 11.

28. H. Brunner, *Die Weisheitsbücher der Ägypter* (Zurich: Artemis, 1991) 14: "It would therefore be completely wrong to impute purely secular motives to the instructions and place these in opposition to religion. Profane and religious do not exclude each other, Maat belongs to both sphere."

29. M. L. Barre, "'Fear of God' and the World View of Wisdom," *Biblical Theology Bulletin 11* (1981) 41-43.

30. A leading exponent of this view is H. D. Preuss, *Einführung in die alttestamentliche Literatur* (Urbantaschenbücher 383; Stuttgart: Kohlhammer, 1987) 60, 163.

31. Murphy, *The Tree of Life*, 8.

32. On the topic, see R. N. Whybray, "Poverty, Wealth, and Point of View in Proverbs," *The Expository Times* 100 (1989) 333-36; R. 4 Van Leeuwen, "Wealth and Poverty: System and Contradiction in Proverbs," *Hebrew Studies* 33 (1992) 25-36.

33. M. Lichtheim, *Ancient Egyptian Literature* (Berkeley: University of California, 1976) II.176 (4.7-10 in the manuscript).

34. New York: Paulist, 1994.

35. Ibid., 41.

36. Also Prov 3:13-26 and 8:32-35.

37. For a convenient summary of much of the recent discussion, see B. Witherington, *Jesus the Sage: The Pilgrimage of Wisdom* (Philadelphia: Fortress, 1994).

The Père Marquette Lectures in Theology

1969 *The Authority for Authority*
        Quentin Quesnell
        Professor of Theology
        Marquette University

1970 *Mystery and Truth*
        John Macquarrie
        Professor of Theology
        Union Theological Seminary

1971 *Doctrinal Pluralism*
        Bernard Lonergan, S.J.
        Professor of Theology
        Regis College, Ontario

1972 *Infallibility*
        George A. Lindbeck
        Professor of Theology
        Yale University

1973 *Ambiguity in Moral Choice*
        Richard A. McCormick, S.J.
        Professor of Moral Theology
        Bellarmine School of Theology

1974 *Church Membership as a Catholic and
Ecumenical Problem*
        Avery Dulles, S.J.
        Professor of Theology
        Woodstock College

1975 *The Contributions of Theology to Medical Ethics*
James Gustafson
University Professor of Theological Ethics
University of Chicago

1976 *Religious Values in an Age of Violence*
Rabbi Marc Tannenbaum
Director of National Interreligious Affairs
American Jewish Committee, New York City

1977 *Truth Beyond Relativism:*
Karl Mannheim's Sociology of Knowledge
Gregory Baum
Professor of Theology and Religious Studies
St. Michael's College

1978 *A Theology of 'Uncreated Energies'*
George A. Maloney, S.J.
Professor of Theology
John XXIII Center for Eastern Christian
Studies
Fordham University

1980 *Method in Theology:*
An Organon For Our Time
Frederick E. Crowe, S.J.
Research Professor in Theology
Regis College, Toronto

1981 *Catholics in the Promised Land of the Saints*
James Hennesey, S.J.
Professor of the History of Christianity
Boston College

THE PÈRE MARQUETTE LECTURES IN THEOLOGY

1982 *Whose Experience Counts in Theological Reflection?*
      Monika Hellwig
      Professor of Theology
      Georgetown University

1983 *The Theology and Setting of Discipleship in the
      Gospel of Mark*
         John R. Donahue, S.J.
         Professor of Theology
         Jesuit School of Theology, Berkeley

1984 *Should War be Eliminated? Philosophical and
      Theological Investigations*
         Stanley Hauerwas
         Professor of Theology
         Notre Dame University

1985 *From Vision to Legislation:
      From the Council to a Code of Laws*
         Ladislas M. Orsy, S.J.
         Professor of Canon Law
         The Catholic University of America

1986 *Revelation and Violence:
      A Study in Contextualization*
         Walter Brueggemann
         Professor of Old Testament
         Eden Theological Seminary
         St. Louis, Missouri

MARQUETTE UNIVERSITY

1987 *Nova et Vetera:*
   The Theology of Tradition in American Catholicism
      Gerald Fogarty
      Professor of Religious Studies
      University of Virginia

1988 *The Christian Understanding of Freedom and the*
   History of Freedom in the Modern Era:
   The Meeting and Confrontation Between
   Christianity and the Modern Era in a Postmodern
   Situation
      Walter Kasper
      Professor of Dogmatic Theology
      University of Tübingen

1989 *Moral Absolutes: Catholic Tradition, Current*
   Trends, and the Truth
      William F. May
      Ordinary Professor of Moral Theology
      Catholic University of America

1990 *Is Mark's Gospel a Life of Jesus? The Question of*
   Genre
      Adela Yarbro Collins
      Professor of New Testament
      University of Notre Dame

1991 *Faith, History and Cultures:*
   Stability and Change in Church Teachings
      Walter H. Principe, C.S.B.
      Professor of Theology
      University of Toronto

Uniform format, cover, and binding.
Copies of this Lecture and the others in the series are
obtainable from:

Marquette University Press
Marquette University
Milwaukee WI 53201-1881 U.S.A.

(414) 288-1564   (414) 288-3300 (fax)
University and Book Store Purchase Orders. Visa, MasterCard,
Discover, American Express.